Getting into Ovation

by Roger Amos

Getting into Ovation
Roger Amos
Edited by David Bradforth
© RISC Developments Ltd. 1994

ISBN-13: 978-1517359676 (CreateSpace-Assigned)
ISBN-10: 1517359678

Third edition September 2015
Second edition April 2001
First printed in the UK April 1994

This book was produced on an Acorn Archimedes 32-bit computer. It was writted and edited using APDL/ProAction's *Ovation DTP* package, and subsequently typeset using David Pilling's Ovation Pro DTP package. This edition has been manipulated using *InDesign* for publishing on Amazon.

Published by
Alligata Media, 16 Rodney Way, Romford, Essex RM7 8PD
email dave.bradforth@gmail.com

Printed by CreateSpace, an Amazon.com company.

Contents

3 Planning your document   35

4 Other facilities   45

Introduction

Since you are reading this booklet, presumably you (or your school) have bought, or perhaps are seriously considering buying, Ovation. You want to know you how to get results from this software package - and quickly.

What Ovation is

Ovation is a fully comprehensive DeskTop Publishing (DTP) package. It allows you to produce documents which use industry-standard typefaces - not just those resident in your printer - and which include graphics (diagrams and pictures) as well as text. It is nevertheless remarkably easy to use, since what you see on the screen accurately represents the appearance of your document when printed.

It is exceptionally versatile. You may use it as a word processor to produce simple documents like letters and memos. And you may use it to produce more complex ones such as posters, magazines and newspapers with multiple-column layouts and incorporating pictures as well as text. This book was written using Ovation, and the first version of it was designed using Ovation.

Ovation also incorporates a mail merge facility which allows you to generate personalised letters automatically. So, if you are a teacher, you could use Ovation to send personalised letters to the parents or guardians of all the pupils in your class. If you are in business you can send personalised letters to your customers. A club or church could send personalised letters to its members. The possibilities are endless.

Add to that a spelling checker and the option of a direct link to David Pilling's Desktop Thesaurus and you will find that Ovation is invaluable if you need to produce documents of any description.

What you need

To use Ovation, you will require a computer running RISC OS 3.1 or later. These may have a number of brandings, most likely Acorn/Castle Technology, MicroDigital or RiscStation. You may also be running RISC OS on a PC/Mac under Virtual Acorn. We also assume that you have 4Mb of RAM or greater, as to use a DTP application to its full you will require a reasonable amount of memory.

The latest release of Ovation is available as a free download from the apdl.org.uk website. Purchasers of Getting into Ovation will be able to find this at www.apdl. org.uk/books/gio. The source code is available on David Pilling's website.

What this book does

This book is a quick guide to the main features offered by Ovation. It is not fully comprehensive; not all of the facilities are described. But if you only need to learn the essentials of the package, perhaps because you need to produce a document quickly, this booklet will help you.

Chapter 1 tells you about typing and editing text and importing text from other software packages. It also covers text styles and formatting text.

Chapter 2 tells you about the text frames, picture frames and lines that make up an Ovation document.

Chapter 3 tells you about facilities that help to keep your documents consistent and provide short-cuts: these include master pages, chapters, paragraph styles and stylesheets.

Chapter 4 covers a few of the other facilities such as the spelling checker, the link to Desktop Thesaurus and lastly how to print your document and how to use the mail merge option.

We have assumed in this book that you are familiar with some standard RISC OS conventions. The most essential is that the three mouse buttons are, from left to right, Select, Menu and Adjust. If you require further guidance, please refer to the RISC OS manual.

Installing Ovation

To install Ovation, double-click on the !Install application contained within the download file. You'll first be required to drag the application icon into the directory you wish Ovation to be installed. Do this only from the installer window: it will not work any other way. The installer will prompt you for the name you wish to register Ovation under - type this in and click OK to allow the installation to continue.

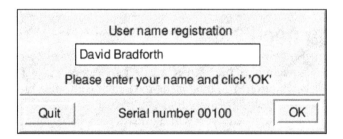

Once you double click on the !Install application, you'll be prompted for a user name. This will be placed into the program template upon installation as well as a serial number. This should be quoted in all technical support queries with APDL/ProAction.

Starting up Ovation

Ovation follows the standard conventions for RISC OS. To load the application display the directory containing the !Ovation application and double-click Select or Adjust on the program icon. The application will be loaded into memory and its icon will appear on the iconbar, but no document window will be opened. If you double-clicked Adjust the directory display will now be closed.

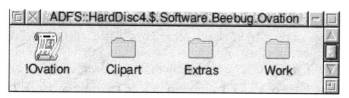

A directory display showing Ovation alongside its various resource directories.

Loading an existing Ovation document

Open a directory containing an Ovation document file and double click on it. Provided that the computer has seen the !Ovation application a window will be opened showing the start of the document.

If the document contains some fonts which are not present on your system, the program will tell you this and ask if you wish to continue loading it - click yes or no to continue.

A4_60x72	WR/	1718	OvnStyle	08:50:03 27 Jul 1992
Chapter1	WR/	18K	Ovation	12:02:58 16 Jun 1990
DraftDoc	WR/	6K	Ovation	08:52:28 27 Jul 1992
Features	WR/	8K	Ovation	12:14:47 16 Jun 1990
Grapevine	/		Directory	21:56:26 11 May 1997
LE_60x72	WR/	1718	OvnStyle	08:50:25 27 Jul 1992
MergeDoc	WR/	4086	Ovation	14:07:51 22 Jul 1992
SampleCSV	WR/	338	CSV	14:02:36 22 Jul 1992
Styles	WR/	3620	Ovation	14:07:00 28 Jun 1990

DFS::HardDisc4.$.Software.Beebug.Ovation.Work.Documents

A directory display showing an Ovation stylesheet (top of the list), various Ovation documents, a directory and a CSV file. Double-clicking on either the OvnStyle documents or the Ovation documents will launch Ovation.

Menus and keystrokes

Ovation makes extensive use of menus and nearly all of the operations available can be accessed by making choices from the menus. For newcomers to Ovation or to Desktop Publishing these provide a simple and logical means of finding your way around the package. Many operations, however, can also be accessed by a keystroke.

Some use the numbered Function keys (F4, for example, is Find/Replace). Others use combinations of the Ctrl key with other keys (Ctrl-C, for example, copies marked text to the clipboard) and others use Shift and Ctrl in conjunction with other keys (Shift-Ctrl-C, for example, centres the marked text). The complete list of function keys is given on the Ovation reference card, included within your package.

These are much faster than using the menu system and you will gradually learn them (most keystroke equivalents are marked on the menus). But to begin with you may prefer to use the menus where the operations are described fully.

This book is not meant as an alternative User Guide and you will need to refer to the User Guide for further information on many topics. Some menus, such as the View menu, are not covered exhaustively. But these are fairly self-explanatory and you will quickly become familiar with their use. The View menu, as its name suggests, is concerned with the screen display and includes zoom options (the size at which the document is displayed on your monitor) and facilities to turn guidelines and rulers on and off.

1 Typing your Text

So you have started up Ovation and you have a window open which is empty apart from a rectangular box (called a text frame) with a small red square (called a handle) at each corner and in the middle of each side. In the top left-hand corner of the text frame is the caret - a red 'I'-shaped cursor. The text frame marks the edges of the area in which you can type.

Apart from the chapter and page numbers and the row of tools in its bottom left-hand corner, the window is an absolutely standard RISC OS window. If you are still using RISC OS 2, there is one exceptional feature that is not immediately obvious. You can drag the window over the right and bottom edges of the screen. This may be useful to you if you want to look at some other window that your Ovation window has covered up. The use of the tools will be covered in the next chapter. The text entry tool, the one on the left containing a caret-shaped icon, should be highlighted (i.e. shown in black with its icon in white) indicating that Ovation is in its text-entry mode.

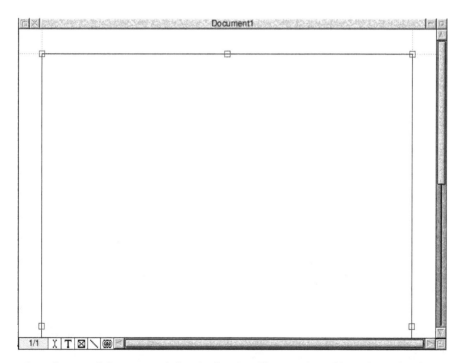

A newly opened document window in Ovation. The caret is visible in the top left-hand corner. In the bottom left-hand corner are the chapter and page numbers and then, from left-to-right, the Ovation tools: text entry, text frame, picture frame, line and link

Typing

Try typing a few words and you will find that the text appears at the caret which then moves to the right. Almost certainly the text you type will initially be in either the supplied font 'SwissB' or 'Homerton' (as supplied with your computer), depending on the contents of the !Fonts directory. We shall see shortly how to change to a different font.

Typing works in the same way as in a word processor. When the caret reaches the end of the line, a new line is started automatically - you do not need to press the Return key unless you are deliberately starting a new paragraph or leaving a blank line. If the end of the line falls in the middle of a word, as often happens, the word break is handled automatically, the broken word usually being carried over to the new line, and the first part of it erased from the previous line. It all happens so quickly you will probably not be aware that it is happening.

Similarly, when you get to the end of the first page, a new page is started automatically. You can force the start of a new page at any time by pressing the Enter key, the bottom key at the right-hand corner of the numeric keypad.

You can use the cursor keys to move the caret around. If you move the caret into the midst of text that you have typed and you type some more characters, these will be inserted at the caret's new position. Text to the right of the caret will move to the right automatically to make room for the new material.

Using special characters

Your document may need to include special characters which are available in the fonts but which cannot be typed on the keyboard in the normal way. Examples are the accented letters (such as é and ï) and other special symbols such as ", ˜, œ, © and ®. There are two ways in which you can use these characters. If you know the ASCII code for the character (each character is represented by a number between 0 and 255) hold down either Alt key and type the code number on the numeric keypad. When you release the Alt key the required character will appear at the caret. For example, to type é (code 233), hold down Alt, on the numeric keypad type 2, followed by 3, followed by another 3 and then release Alt. You will find a Table of the characters with their ASCII codes in the Ovation User Manual.

Alternatively use the Chars application in the Resources directory in RISC OS or the provided Charsel application supplied with Ovation. This displays all the characters in the font in a window; move the pointer over the character you wish to type and click Select. Remember to take the pointer out of the window before you return to normal typing, or Charsel will remain active and may interfere with your typing.

Moving the caret around

As we have seen, you can move the caret around by means of the cursor keys. The left and right keys move the caret one character forwards and backwards. If you hold down Shift they move the caret to the start of the previous or next word. If you hold down Ctrl they move the caret to the start or end of the line.

The up and down keys move the caret up or down a line. You will not, however, be able to take the caret above the first line of text or below the last line. If you hold down Shift they move the caret to the start of the previous or next paragraph; (a blank line counts as a paragraph in Ovation as in other packages). If you hold down Ctrl they move the caret to the start or end of the text you are typing. The Home key also takes the caret to the start of the text.

If you move the mouse within the text frame, you will find it moves a black 'I'-shaped pointer around the text, while the caret stays where you left it. If you click Select, the caret will move to the position of this pointer. This provides a quick method of moving the caret to any point where you wish to work.

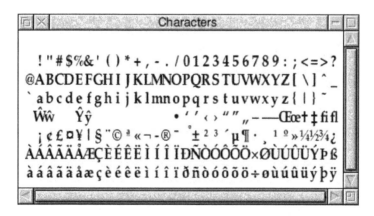

The complete display of the Paladin.Bold font in !Chars.

Changing the view

The documents you create in Ovation are likely to get too long to fit within a single screen display. If the top part of the document scrolls off the screen you can drag the scroll bar upwards (move the pointer on to it, hold down Select and move it upwards) to get the top of the document back on screen.

Alternatively you can use the Page Up and Page Down keys to step the 'view' (the visible portion of the document) backwards and forwards through the document. Using these keys while Shift is held down will step backwards or forwards one page. While Ctrl is held down they will move to the first and last pages of the document. There is also a Goto Page facility (press Ctrl-G or F5) in which you enter the number of the page you wish to see; this is a fast means of moving around a long document as the computer does not have to redraw each intermediate page.

These operations do not affect the caret; it remains wherever you left it and it may be off the screen. If you wish to type or edit text in a screen which does not contain the caret, you must first place the pointer where you want the caret and click Select to move the caret there. If you omit to do this and you press a character key or one of the arrowed cursor keys, the character will be typed at the present caret position or the caret will be moved one step, even though it is off screen, but the view will be changed immediately to bring the area around the caret back on screen.

Selecting material

Many operations require a portion of text to be selected (or 'marked') for special attention. You may wish to move it elsewhere in the document, to save it as a separate file, to delete it or to change it to a different font or style. Marked text is highlighted by inverse video, i.e. the text is shown in paper colour (usually white) against a background that is ink colour (usually black), thus: `marked text.`

There are several ways to mark portions of text in Ovation. To select an individual word, place the caret anywhere in it and double-click Select, i.e. click Select twice in quick succession. The word (and any spaces that immediately follow it) will be marked. To select a line of text place the caret anywhere in it and treble-click select. The whole line will be marked. To select a whole paragraph place the caret anywhere in it and quadruple-click Select. The whole paragraph will be marked. To select all the text click Select five times. Alternatively click Menu, move right on second entry in the main menu, Edit and click on the first item in the Edit menu, Select All. In some versions of Ovation this facility is also available by pressing Ctrl-A; in some versions you must use the right-hand Ctrl key. It is also available by pressing Ctrl-O; this is useful for users of the A4 portable computer which does not have a right-hand Ctrl key. All of the body of text containing the caret (the currently active story) will be marked. Your document may contain other portions of text that are not part of the current story; we shall learn about these in the next two chapters. These will not be affected by Select All.

There are two ways in which you may select a passage of text which might begin and end anywhere, even in the middle of a word. Both methods involve using the mouse. Move the pointer to one end of the passage to be marked, press Select and hold it down and drag (i.e. move the pointer while still holding down Select) to the other end of the passage and then release Select. The passage will be marked. Alternatively place the caret at one end of the passage to be marked, move the pointer to the other end and click Adjust. The passage will again be marked.

Note that the caret disappears while a passage is marked. You can adjust the length of any marked passage by moving the pointer to the place where you want it to start or end and clicking Adjust. To unmark a marked section and return it to normal text click Select anywhere in the text or press any of the cursor keys or press Ctrl-Z. The marked section is restored to normal and the caret reappears.

Deleting material

Ovation offers several methods for deleting unwanted text. To delete the character to the left of the caret press Delete or Backspace. To delete the character to the right of the caret press Copy. Following either of these deletions text to the right of the caret will move to the left to close the gap.

To delete the word containing the caret press Shift-Delete. To delete the line containing the caret press Ctrl-Delete. To delete a marked area of text press Delete. If the text is more than 50 characters long you will be prompted to confirm that you wish to proceed with the deletion. This is an important precaution since text deleted in this way cannot be retrieved.

To replace the marked area of text with new material simply begin typing the new material. The marked area of text will disappear and be replaced by the caret and your new material will be typed in the normal way. But if the marked area is more than 50 characters long, you will be prompted to confirm the deletion after typing the first character. Any characters you typed after the first character but before confirming the deletion will be lost.

Alternatively, you can cut the marked text using the Cut Text option in the Edit menu or by pressing Ctrl-X (the same keypress as in Acorn Edit). Although the marked text disappears from the screen you will not be prompted to confirm the operation since the text is not lost irretrievably; it has been transferred to a reserved area of memory called the clipboard from which it can be reclaimed (until you store something else on the clipboard).

Copying and moving text

Copying and moving text use of the clipboard which we have just met. There are four menu options in the Edit menu that affect the clipboard. Each has a short-cut keypress which is the same as the equivalent operation in Acorn Edit.

Cut Text (Ctrl-X), as we have seen, removes the marked text from the document and places it on the clipboard. Copy Text (Ctrl-C) leaves the marked text unchanged, but makes a copy of it on the clipboard. Both of these operations overwrite any material already on the clipboard; no warning is given. Paste Text (Ctrl-V) copies the text on the clipboard into the document at the caret position. The clipboard contents, however, are unchanged and so may be copied into another part of the document as many times as necessary. Show Clipboard (Ctrl-B) opens a window showing the current contents of the clipboard and is useful if you have forgotten what it contains.

If your computer has enough memory, you may have up to six Ovation documents open simultaneously, but there is only one clipboard which is common to all of them. So material cut or copied from one document can be pasted into another or several other documents. The clipboard is a very simple method of transferring material between documents.

Find and replace

If you have used a word processor or a text editor such as Edit you will probably be familiar with Find-and-Replace facilities. Ovation offers a comprehensive facility for this purpose; to use it select Find/Replace in the Edit menu or press Ctrl-F or F4.

Enter what you wish to search for in the Find: box and press Return. This places the caret in Replace: box where you enter the string with which you to wish to replace it (if any). To set the search in motion, click Select on Find. The search normally begins at the caret position, so that any occurrences above the caret will not be found. You can force the search to begin at the start by clicking on Find from Start before clicking on Find.

The Find and Replace dialogue box.

If an occurrence of the Find string is found, the view changes (if necessary) so that it is on screen and it is highlighted, i.e. marked. Further action is up to you. If you wish to replace it with the Replace string, click in Replace. (If there is no replace string Replace will delete the highlighted text). If you wish to replace it and find the next occurrence click in Replace/Find. If you wish to leave this occurrence unchanged and find further occurrences, click again in Find. If you inadvertently replace an occurrence that should have been left unchanged, clicking in Undo immediately afterwards will restore that occurrence. To abandon the Find/Replace operation, click in Cancel, which closes the dialogue box.

Clicking in Global Replace after entering the Find string and Replace string will force the automatic replacement of every occurrence of the search string with the Replace string; you will have no opportunity to check that these replacements are indeed the ones you intended. You can, however, restrict the part of the text you wish to search by marking it; if there is marked text present, Global Replace is confined to this.

Clicking in Count simply counts the occurrences of the search string in the area being searched.

There are some useful options in the Find/Replace facility. Whole Word will only find the Find string if it exists as a whole word, i.e. bounded by spaces or punctuation marks. If this option is not selected the string will be found whether it occurs as a word or as part of a longer word.

Ignore Case allows matches to be made even if the use of capitals and lower-case letters is different. In the replace string the usage of capitals and lower-case will follow that of the text replaced.

Wildcards allows special characters to be used in the Find string (but not the Replace string). These characters are preceded by the backslash character '\'. The most useful wildcards are as follows. * represents any single character. Thus if you enter 'b*t' as the Find string, 'bat', 'bet', 'bit' and 'but' would all be found. \t represents the Tab character and \p represents the Return (new paragraph) character. \ \ represents the backslash character itself.

Fonts, sizes and other text styles

DTP packages like Ovation allow you to use a virtually limitless range of typefaces, typesizes and special effects. You can use almost any symbol or any effect available in professional printing houses. You are not restricted to the typefaces resident in your printer since the same outline fonts that you see on the screen are also used for printing, the text being printed as though it were graphics. If you use a PostScript® printer, you will need to download into it copies of any outline fonts you are using which have no equivalents in its resident font set.

To change font, size or style you will need to click Menu. This calls up Ovation's main menu of 11 items. Each option leads to a further menu. The three of interest to us are the fifth, sixth and seventh in the main menu.

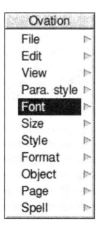

The Fonts menu consists of a list of the outline font families present in your !Fonts directory, in alphabetical order. A selection of outline fonts is supplied with RISC OS 3 and a further selection is supplied with Ovation. Other fonts are available from software houses, but those from public-domain sources are likely to be of inferior quality. Ovation places no restriction on the number of fonts it will work with; the only limitation is the disc storage space available for the directory. If there are more fonts than will fit on the menu, a scroll bar allows you to scroll through the list. A tick will appear by the font in use at the caret, or if there is marked text present, by the first font used in the marked text.

The main menu

Fonts
Arial
Arial Medium
Arial Black
Arial Condensed
Arial ExtraBold
Arial Light
Arial Condensed ExtraBold
Arial
Arial Condensed Light
Arial Rounded ExtraBold
Avonair
Bookmark
Brushscrip

A typical font menu in Ovation. The font Bookmark has been selected.

To select a new font from the list simply click Select or Adjust on it; the tick will now appear by this font. If there is marked text present, it will be changed to the font you selected. If there is no marked text present, new text typed at the caret will be in the newly selected font.

The Size menu offers a range of popular type sizes: 8, 10, 12, 14, 18, 24 and 36 pt (points). A point is exactly 1/72 inch and the font size is the range of height it covers, i.e. the distance from the tip of the tallest character (probably a 'b' or 'd') to the tip of the longest descender (probably a 'p' or 'q').

There is also at the foot of the menu an item marked Other Size. If you wish to use a size not included in the menu, such as 9 pt or 30.75 pt, follow the arrow on this item to a dialogue box in which you can write your choice of size. Ovation accepts all sizes from 1 to 1000 pt; fractional sizes are permitted but are rounded to the nearest 1/16 pt.

In other respects the Size menu works like the Fonts menu. A tick appears by the size used in any marked text or the text around the caret. Choosing a new size by clicking on it applies that size to any marked text; if there is no marked text it applies it to the next text you type.

The Style menu is more complex than the Fonts or Size menu. Some of its 16 items lead to writable icons, which affect the form or position of the text. Unlike the Fonts and Size menus, the items are not all mutually exclusive: you can only have one font and one size selected, but you can have several simultaneous styles selected. For instance, you could have bold, italic, underline, superscript and reverse all selected and therefore ticked simultaneously; you are unlikely ever to need that particular combination of styles, but it is nevertheless a legitimate choice. Many options are toggle switches: clicking on the option selects it and places a tick by it; clicking on it again deselects it and the tick disappears.

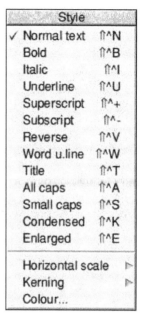

Selecting the Normal option cancels all other style selections from this menu except colour. It is the default, printing the standard form of the text. Bold prints a bold, thick-looking version of the typeface, useful for headings and emphasis. Note that Ovation recognises several different terms for 'bold': 'demi' and 'black' are both regarded as equivalent to 'bold'. Italic selects italic or oblique script used for emphasis or quotations or names.

The Style menu in Ovation

Note that the bold and italic effects depend on the presence in the !Fonts directory of suitably named fonts. If there is no such font, the selection is ignored. If, for instance, you are using the Chaucer font and you select bold, there will be no change since there is no bold version of this font.

Underline places a line beneath all the text affected, including spaces. Superscript and Subscript are mutually exclusive. Both produce text that is approximately half the current size. In superscript it is positioned above the line as in mathematical powers, e.g. $2^8 = 256$. Subscript is written below the line and is often used in chemical formulae, e.g. H_2SO_4. You can use superscript and subscript together to produce fractions with or without a (condensed) oblique: $1\frac{1}{2}, 2\frac{3}{4}$.

Reverse changes the text colour to the paper colour and vice versa. It is useful for certain special effects, especially in software user manuals where it is often used to indicate certain keys such as F1 and Esc. It looks best with a bold typeface. Please note that this effect cannot at present be reproduced on dot-matrix printers.

Word Underline is mutually exclusive with underline. It underlines only the words, leaving spaces unaffected.

Title and All Caps are also mutually exclusive. All Caps forces all the affected text to appear in capital letters only. Title, useful for titles and headings, forces the first letter of each word to appear in capitals and the rest in lower case.

Small Caps replaces all lower-case letters in the affected text with capitals of approximately three quarters the normal size. Capitals themselves are unaffected, So You Can Mix Normal Capitals and Small Capitals.

Condensed, Enlarged and Horizontal Scale are again mutually exclusive; they affect the width of the text being used. Condensed squeezes the text so that it is only 60% of its normal width. This is useful where you need to accommodate a lot of text in a confined space. Enlarged is the opposite of Condensed; the text is double its normal width, useful for headings where space does not permit a larger (taller) type size. Horizontal Scale allows you to enter the scaling factor of your choice; you could use it to produce very condensed or greatly expanded text, but these are not easy to read. It is particularly useful where a heading is just too long to fit in one line, but you do not wish to split it into two lines; sometimes horizontal scaling to, say, 98% - the change is imperceptible - allows you to fit the text in one line.

Kerning and Tracking (the menu item reads Tracking if there is marked text and Kerning at other times) affect the spacing between adjacent characters. Kerning applies to an individual pair of characters and tracking to longer passages of text. For example, the shape of the letters 'W' and 'A' creates the impression of a noticeable gap between them when they are adjacent: WA. To kern a pair of letters place the caret between them, select the Kerning option and enter a value between -500 and 500. Negative values move the characters closer and positive values space them out. A value of -150 gives the following result which looks better: WA. Tracking allows you to squeeze any group of characters closer together, but this can make text difficult to read.

Colour allows you to change the colour of the text. A standard palette of 16 colours is offered and you can either choose one of these or formulate your own colour using the red, green and blue sliders. If you formulate your own colour, the computer will use the closest available colour from the current palette when reproducing your text on the screen or may use a dither pattern (a pattern in which alternate pixels have different colours) to simulate the colour you have chosen. If you print your document using a colour printer, the full colour information will be sent to the printer and it will use the closest match of which it is capable.

All changes of Font, Size and Style are applied only to the marked text if any is present; if none is present they are applied to any new text typed. There will probably be occasions when you wish to change the font and size and select styles all at the same time. It is quickest to make all except the last selection by clicking with Adjust, since this leaves the menu structure open and delays making any actual changes on the screen. Click Select on the final selection. This closes the menus and rewrites any selected text in the new font, size and style. (If you click Select after each selection you will not only need to reopen the menu each time, but also the computer will rewrite the text each time, which slows down the operations appreciably.)

Formatting your text

The Font, Size and Style menus are concerned with the appearance of text, but not the way in which it is laid out. That is controlled by the Format menu.

The first four items are mutually exclusive and are concerned with the alignment of the text on its line. Left gives a straight left-hand margin and a ragged right-hand margin, as on a conventional typewriter. It is useful for writing letters and in documents having narrow columns.

Centre centres the text between the margins and is most useful in headings. Right pushes the text to the right, so that it has a straight right-hand margin and a ragged left-hand margin. Justify makes both left-hand and right-hand margins straight by expanding the spaces between words; it is the format with which we are most familiar from books and newspapers.

The next five options are concerned with the vertical spacing between lines. Most critical is Leading which takes its name from the days when printers used strips of lead alloy to space out lines of type. You should usually have some space between lines, because this makes it easier for the eyes to find their way from the end of one line to start of the next. Only in newspaper-style formats where the columns are very narrow may you be able to 'set solid' (to use printers' jargon), that is, have no leading (empty space) between the lines.

Leading can be expressed in absolute terms, incremental terms or relative terms. The most useful method of expressing leading is relative leading which is in the form of a percentage. The default setting in Ovation is 20%. With 10 pt type the leading will be 20% of 10 i.e. 2 pt. The advantage is that if you change the typesize, the leading changes in proportion, keeping the ratio of type to white space constant.

In absolute leading you enter a figure in points, e.g. 12 pt. You might have type of size 10 pt with a leading of 12 pt. This also puts 2 pt of white space between lines. But if you subsequently change the typesize to, say 14 pt, the leading will remain 12 pt and the lines of type will overlap each other, which is untidy and very difficult to read. If you use absolute leading, you must remember to set the leading to a sensible value for the current type size.

Incremental leading is usually preceded by a + sign, e.g. +2 pt. This sets the leading to the present type size plus the relative setting. So if you are using 12 pt type with a relative leading of +2 pt, the actual leading will be 12 + 2 = 14 pt. The advantage of relative leading is that if you subsequently change the size of the type to, say, 14 pt there will still be 2 pt of leading between lines.

Single Space and Double Space set the leading to the default of 20% and to 100% leading respectively.

Space Before and Space After relate to paragraphs, allowing you to insert extra space before or after paragraphs so that paragraph breaks stand out. By careful use of these facilities you can also ensure that columns of text are all the same height.

Tabs/Indents controls a variety of text formatting functions which are set from a dialogue box and a ruler (Figure 1.8). The ruler spans the currently active text frame and is calibrated so that measurements begin where text begins, that is, at the left hand edge of the frame plus the inset. It shows the current positions of all tab stops and indents. All positioning of tab stops and indents uses these measurements, relative to the position of the text frame.

If you are familiar with Tab stops on a conventional typewriter, you will know that when you have set your tab stops, pressing the Tab key moves the carriage immediately to the next tab position and this makes the creation of tabular information very quick and easy. The same applies in Ovation but you have many additional facilities. There are four kinds of tab stop. Left tabs are like those on typewriters: when you move to a left tab the text you type starts at the tab position. When you move to a right tab, the text you type extends to the left of it so that it ends on the tab. When you move to a centre tab, the text extends equally left and right of it so that its centre is on the tab. Decimal tabs are often used for displaying sums of money in financial documents; the decimal points (between the pounds and pence or dollars and cents) are aligned on the decimal tab stop so that the figures appear in the correct columns.

You can mix tab stops of different types, although you are unlikely to need to do so. When typing your document, a press on the Tab key will move the caret onwards to the next tab stop of whatever kind.

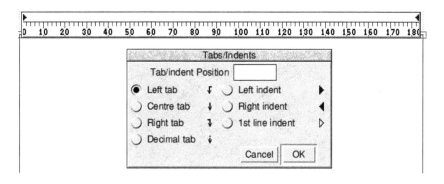

The Tabs/Indents dialogue box and its associated ruler. In the illustrated example, the tabs/indents have yet to be set, and the ruler is for the width of an A4 page.

To set tab stops, click on the radio button for the kind of tab you wish to set and then click Select on the ruler at the appropriate point. You may adjust the position of a tab stop by dragging it with Select or by entering the tab position in the writable field. You must terminate the entry for each tab stop by pressing Return or your entry will be ignored. To remove a tab stop, drag it down off the ruler.

This is a demonstration of the tabulator in *Ovation*. There is a left tab at 25mm, a centre tab at 50mm, a right tab at 75mm and a decimal tab at 100mm.

ABC	ABC	ABC	0.10
ABCD	ABCD	ABCD	12.25
ABCDE	ABCDE	ABCDE	.03

The effect of the four types of tab in Ovation

Although they are not shown on the ruler, there are default tab stops. Left-hand tabs are set automatically at 10 mm intervals across the text frame. You may find that these are perfectly adequate for your requirements.

Three indents are provided and they work exactly like tab stops. The left and right indents determine the normal left-hand and right-hand limits of text and are at the edge of the frame, less the inset. You may reposition either to suit your requirements. The first-line indent applies a separate left indent to the first line of paragraphs only. It allows you to indent the first line of each paragraph or to set a 'hanging indent' in which the first-line indent is set to 0, while the left indent is set to a different value, indenting the remaining lines of the paragraph.

Word Wrap is normally turned on. It is the facility that ensures that words are not broken at the ends of lines. You may on occasion, however, disable this facility

This is an example of an indented paragraph. The left indent is 0 and the first-line indent is 10mm.	● This is an example of a hanging indent. The left indent is 10mm and the first-line indent is 0mm.

Use of left and first-line indents

if you are reproducing a computer program listing or a block of data in some special format.

The Hyphenation facility will only operate if your computer has at least 2 Mb of RAM. It is normally disabled, the entire word that would be broken at the end of the line being carried over to the next line. If hyphenation is enabled, Ovation will hyphenate words that fall at the end of the line under certain conditions. You may select the minimum length of word to be hyphenated (the default is 6 letters) and you may choose an option that prevents words that begin with a capital from being hyphenated. See the Ovation User Guide for more details.

Saving your work

To save your document for the first time, click Menu and choose the first option from the main menu, File. Follow the arrow on the second item, Save as. Alternatively press F3. This leads to a standard Save dialogue box. Enter a filename (or accept the one offered) and drag the icon into your choice of directory viewer, and the document will be saved in that directory. The computer will remember the filename and the directory and you may in future save the file whenever you wish by clicking on the first option in the File menu, Save, or by pressing Ctrl-S or F3 followed by Return.

You are advised to save your work regularly in case a power failure or some other catastrophe should destroy it; an Auto Save facility in the File menu saves your work at regular intervals (the default being 10 minutes). Its use is recommended; when catastrophe strikes at worst you will have lost only a few minutes' work.

This form of Save saves all the document data, so that when you subsequently reload the document, it will look exactly as it did when you saved it.

Importing text

Much of this chapter has been concerned with the typing of text. You may not need to type much text. If you already have the text as a text file, you can import it straight into Ovation. If it is a plain text file as created by Acorn Edit, all you need to do is to drag the file out of its directory display into the position in your Ovation document. If the caret is visible, the new text will be inserted at the caret; otherwise it will be placed where you dragged it. The text will then appear in your document just as though you had typed it on the keyboard. Incidentally Ovation makes a few subtle changes to text imported in this way. The old-fashioned single and double quotation marks (' and ") are automatically replaced by the more attractive open and close quotes (' and ', " and •) as appropriate.

You may find that the line breaks are now at inappropriate points, where they were broken in the application that created the file which probably used a different font and line length. If this happens, delete the imported text and drag the file into Ovation again, but this time hold down the Ctrl key at the same time. The line breaks will be replaced by regular spaces. You may now find that paragraphs have run together; these will need separating with the Return key, but that is far easier than manually correcting individual lines of the wrong length.

Text imported from Edit and other text editors will of course contain no details concerning fonts, sizes or styles.

If you are using version 1.30 (or later) of Ovation you can also import documents created by the word processor 1st Word Plus. These must be dragged on to the Ovation icon on the icon bar so that they form new Ovation documents; they cannot be dragged into existing Ovation documents. Font information, underline, subscript and superscript styles, new paragraphs, new pages and hyphen information will all be preserved.

Exporting text

You can also save your Ovation story as a plain text file. From the File menu select the option Save as Text and save in the normal way. You can also save any portion of the story by marking it first and selecting the Save Marked Text option. The text file saved in either operation will consist of plain text and will carry no information regarding fonts or styles.

This facility may be useful to you if you wish to transfer your document into a different software package or even to a different computer system. For example, if you save the text file on an MS-DOS disc, most PC word processors will be able to import the document.

2 Using the Tools

One of the differences between a DTP package like Ovation and a word processor is that the DTP package allows you to include many separate stories (items of text) in your document. It also allows you to include graphics, such as pictures and diagrams, although some modern word processors also handle graphics. Indeed, your document may incorporate any of the features that you are accustomed to seeing in magazines and newspapers.

The Ovation tools, which we met briefly at the beginning of the last chapter, are used extensively in page design. These are the five icons near the bottom left-hand corner of the Ovation window. From left to right, they are the text entry tool (containing a caret), the text frame tool (containing a letter T), the picture frame tool (containing a square with diagonals), the line tool (containing an oblique line) and the link tool (containing three links of a chain). Always one tool or another is selected and shown in inverse video; by default it is the text entry tool. While the text tool is selected, a text frame somewhere in the document is active and contains the caret (or marked text).

Like Acorn's Draw with which you are probably familiar, Ovation is an object-based package; everything that you include in a document is an object or part of an object. Three types of object may be included in an Ovation document: text frames, picture frames and lines. The second, third and fourth tools create these three types of object respectively. The link tool is used to link text frames so that one story is shared between them. We shall look at each of these objects in turn.

Text frames

A text frame, as its name suggests, is a frame or box which can contain text. We met one text frame in the last chapter. It is the rectangle with the eight red handles which appears automatically in a newly opened Ovation document window and on each new page added to the document.

This particular text frame is known as the principal text frame (ptf) and it differs in several important respects from the text frames that you create with the text frame tool. As we have seen, it appears automatically on every page; you do not need to create it. You cannot delete it, cut it or copy it, although you can change its size and you can decide not to use it. Another difference is that the ptf may contain multiple columns of text; we shall see in the next chapter how this is possible. The ptfs in a document (or in one chapter if the document is divided into chapters) are all automatically linked to each other so that the text in them flows between them in one continuous story. For example, if you delete matter on the first page, text will flow back from later pages to fill the gap and if you add new matter on the first page, text will overflow on to later pages and may even cause a new page to be added to the end of the document.

In contrast, each text frame that you create using the text frame tool is initially independent. Any text that you type or import into it forms a story in its own right, quite separate from all other text in the document. Each frame may be deleted, cut or copied ad lib. You may, however, choose to link text frames using the link tool. When two or more text frames are linked, they behave rather like the ptfs in that one story flows between them and they cannot be deleted, cut or copied (unless you first unlink them).

To create a new text frame, click Select on the text frame tool. The pointer changes to a cross-hairs if it is inside the currently active frame. Place the pointer where you want one corner of the frame to be. Hold down Select and drag to where you want the diagonally opposite corner to be; you will drag out a grey "elastic" box as you go. It doesn't matter if you don't get the corner positions exactly right. Now release Select. The sides of the box will turn to black, the eight handles will appear and a caret will appear in the top left-hand corner, ready for you to type or import text. Your new frame has become the active object.

Note that no more than one object at a time in Ovation can be active, that is, can be worked upon. The active object is distinguished by the presence of the red handles. To make another object active, click Select on it. You can make all objects inactive by clicking Select in the margin where you are not over any object.

You can change the size of this (or any) frame by dragging the red handles with Select or Adjust. Dragging a corner handle of course changes both height and width simultaneously; dragging one of the central handles only changes one dimension. If there is text in the frame, you will see the text reformat itself when you change the width of the frame. If you make the frame so small that there is no longer sufficient room in it for all the text, an overflow flag will appear in its bottom right-hand corner.

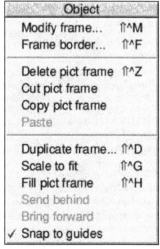

The Object menu

You can also move a frame around by putting the pointer inside it and dragging with Adjust. Note that the edges of the frame will snap on to the edges of other objects it meets and also on to any guidelines that are present. We shall learn in the next Chapter how to lay down these guidelines. If you created the frame so that it was wholly inside another frame (the ptf perhaps) you will find that you cannot drag it outside that frame; it is "trapped" inside it—the technical term is "nested" and this has a special significance which we shall see shortly. If you want to move it outside its parent frame, you must use the cut and paste facilities described later.

The above operations are all inevitably somewhat crude. Ovation does, however, allow you to specify a frame's exact size or exact location. Click on the object to make it active, click Menu and from the main menu select the Object Menu. From this select the first option, Modify Frame. The dialogue box which appears varies depending on the type of frame currently active.

The origin of a text or picture frame is the position of its top left-hand corner. The co-ordinates shown are writable, so you can type a new value if you wish to move the frame to a known location (but you still cannot move it outside a parent frame). To assist you in the accurate placement of objects you can arrange for rulers to appear across the top and along the left-hand side of your Ovation window. From the main menu choose the View menu and click on Show Rulers (which changes to Hide Rulers when the rulers are visible). Another option from the View menu, Units, allows you a choice of inches, millimetres and pts for measurements in the document (but type sizes and leading are always expressed in pts).

The width and height allow you to resize the frame accurately, but you cannot make it so large that it would protrude outside its parent frame if it is nested. The inset and outset are the gap between the edge of the frame and text it contains and text into which it is placed, respectively. The default is 1 mm for both.

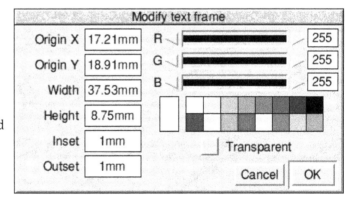

The Modify Text Frame Dialogue Box

The background colour is the "paper colour", the colour behind the text that you type or import. By default it is white, but you can choose any of the 16 palette colours or mix your own colour using the sliders. There is also a transparent option. If you choose this, there will be no colour in the frame and any other objects behind the frame (what this means is discussed later) will remain visible.

Transparency has another special significance which we shall also learn later.

Linking text frames

To link two text frames, click select on the link tool and then move the pointer into the first frame in the linked chain and then drag into the second. If the chain is more than two frames in length, repeat this operation for the second and subsequent links. Whenever you select the link tool, any linkages in the document will be shown symbolically as grey arrows from frame to frame.

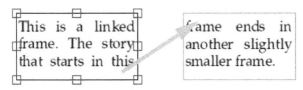

Arrows show the presence and direction
of linkages between frames

You cannot link two frames if both already contain text. You cannot link a frame to itself or to a frame that is already linked. You cannot link a frame to the ptf (which is already linked).

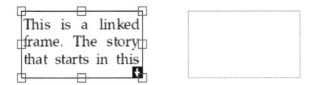

After deleting the link, an overflow flag appears in the first text
frame to show that there is insufficient room for the complete story.

To unlink linked text frames, select the link tool; the grey link arrows will appear as before. Move the pointer over an arrow and click select on it; it turns to black. Now press Delete; the black arrow will disappear and the frames are unlinked. If the first frame is not big enough to contain the full story, an overflow flag will appear.

Picture frames

Picture frames are created in exactly the same way as text frames, but using the picture frame tool. An empty picture frame is distinguished from an empty text frame by the presence of diagonal lines. They behave much as text frames do, but they contain graphics and not text. If you need to place text (such as labels or a caption) in a picture frame in addition to the graphics, you should use separate text frames nested inside the picture frame.

Ovation itself does not contain any facilities to create graphics (apart from lines). But all Ovation users have the applications Paint and Draw which were supplied with RISC OS. Any graphics created with either of these may be imported into an Ovation picture frame. Simply drag the sprite or Drawfile icon from a directory viewer (or straight from the source application's Save dialogue box) into the destination picture frame; it does not need to be the currently active object.

If you have other graphics software and hardware, you may use pictures from these as well, provided that the files are in Acorn sprite format or Drawfile format. So pictures created in art or ray tracing packages or images obtained from scanners and video digitisers can all be imported if in sprite format. Drawings from vector graphics packages such as DrawPlus, Vector and ArtWorks can also be used provided that the files are in the standard Acorn Drawfile format, the objects are all in the default layer and no "foreign" object types are included; objects of unrecognised types are simply ignored and therefore invisible. For example, Vector's replications and radiations must be converted to discrete objects before saving.

You can only have one graphics file at a time in a picture frame. If you drag a new graphics file into a picture frame that already contains a graphic, the new graphic will replace the old one. The old graphic is lost irretrievably (unless you have kept a copy elsewhere) and no warning is given. To empty a picture frame, click Select in it to make it active and choose Delete Picture from the Edit menu (or simply press Delete).

If you select Modify Frame on the Object menu while a picture frame is active a dialogue appears offering the same features as the Modify Text Frame dialogue box, and a few others that relate to the display of graphics.

X scale and Y scale indicate and control the scale at which the

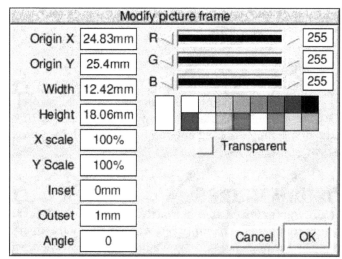

The Modify Picture Frame Dialogue Box

The effect of cropping. Left, a typical family group. Above, the same picture but with the image enlarged and cropped so that only one face appears.

graphic is reproduced. When you first drag a graphics file into a picture frame, Ovation will automatically scale it to the largest possible size that will fit in the frame, but without changing the graphic's aspect ratio; that is to say, it applies the same scaling factor to both horizontal (x) and vertical (y) axes. You may, however, choose to make the image larger or smaller; moreover, you can scale the horizontal and vertical axes independently if you wish so that the image is stretched or squashed.

Ovation allows you to make the graphic so large that it does not fit in the frame (or to resize the frame so that it is smaller than the graphic). This does not set an overflow flag; all that happens is that the part of the graphic that is outside the edge of the frame becomes hidden; you may find it easy to think of the frame as a window through which part of the graphic can be seen. If you move the pointer into the window and press Select, the pointer changes to a push tool (a hand shape) with which you can drag the graphic around and so change the part of it that is visible in the frame. This facility is very useful. For example, if you have a scanned photograph of a group of people only one of whom is of interest in your document, you can make the frame large enough to contain the one person only and then drag the graphic until that person appears centrally in the window, the others being hidden.

Two useful scaling facilities are provided from the Object menu when a picture frame is active. Scale to Fit rescales the graphic making it as large as will fit in the frame, but maintaining the original aspect ratio. Fill Picture Frame also rescales the graphic making it as large as will fit in the frame, but choosing different scaling factors for the two axes, so that the graphic is stretched or squashed as necessary to completely fill the frame.

The angle facility allows you to rotate the graphic about its mid point. You simply enter the number of degrees of anticlockwise rotation. For clockwise either add a minus sign before the figure or subtract the figure from 360.

Lines

Ovation allows you to introduce lines anywhere in your document. Lines are useful in the design of tables and forms and in separating stories and news items in magazine and newspaper design.

All lines are straight: you simply click on the line tool, place the pointer where you want your line to begin, press Select and drag to where you want your line to end. The line is created and becomes the currently active object with a handle at each end.

In many ways the line behaves like a frame. You make a line the currently selected object by clicking on it with Select. You can move the line around by moving the pointer to any position along its length and dragging with Adjust. You can move either end by putting the pointer in the handle and dragging with Select or Adjust.

While a line is active, the Modify Line dialogue box is available from the Object menu. Like the Modify Frame dialogue boxes, it allows you to specify the exact coordinates of the line's two ends (called the Origin and Endpoint) and also its thickness and colour. It also offers a choice of dotted and dashed styles and the option of triangular endcaps on either end or both.

Cutting, copying, pasting and duplicating objects

A number of editing operations that affect whole objects are available from the Object menu. You must first ensure that the object concerned is the active object (it has handles).

The third option in the Object menu, Delete, causes the object to be lost irrevocably. If it is a text frame and it contains text, you will be asked to confirm that you wish to delete the text.

The seventh option, Duplicate, allows you to create a row or column of identical objects at a specified interval. If the original object was nested inside another frame, there must be room in that frame for all the objects being produced. This facility is particularly useful if you are constructing a table and need a series of lines at regular intervals.

In the last chapter we saw how the clipboard can be used to move or copy portions of text around the document or even between documents if you have more than one document open. The clipboard can also hold one frame or one line and can be used to move this from one part of the document to another or between documents. It is the only means of moving an object from one page to another. The fourth, fifth and sixth options in the Object menu use the clipboard and are similar to the corresponding operations with portions of text that we met in the last chapter.

Cut removes the object from the document instantly, but places it on the clipboard. Copy leaves the object unchanged in the document, but makes a copy of it on the clipboard. Either operation will overwrite any matter, text or object, that was previously on the clipboard.

The sixth operation, Paste, is only available if there is an object on the clipboard, otherwise it will be greyed out and unselectable. Paste inserts a copy of the object inside the currently selected object, provided there is room for it. The object remains on the clipboard, however, so you can paste another copy of it elsewhere if you wish.

If the destination object is too small, you will get an error message: "Item too big to paste". Incidentally it is very easy to copy an object to the clipboard, change the view to the destination object and then select Paste, having omitted to click on the destination object to make it active. Ovation will attempt to paste the object inside itself and, not surprisingly, will issue the "Item too big" error. If you get this message when trying to paste a large frame inside the ptf, the fix is to click Select in the margin so that no object is selected. Ovation will then paste the object in the centre of the area of the document in view, where it will be partially outside the ptf. You can then adjust its position to suit your requirements.

Nested objects

When one object is created wholly inside another, it is said to be "nested" in it and is sometimes described as a "child" or "daughter" of the "parent" frame which contains it. Nesting forces a special relationship between the objects. As we have seen, a child frame cannot be dragged outside its parent and can only be removed by cutting or deleting. The child object becomes an integral part of its parent and any operations on the parent object will be applied to the child as well. For example, if the parent is copied or duplicated, the child will be copied or duplicated along with the parent. If the parent is moved, the child will move with the parent. This is useful when dealing with tables and illustrations. A table may contain a collection of lines which are nested objects; these will maintain their correct positions as the table is moved to its required position. An illustration may consist of a picture frame with a nested text frame containing the caption; the caption will always move with the parent picture frame.

If you create a new object wholly or partly outside a larger frame and then drag it inside that frame, it does not become nested. Although inside the larger frame, it remains independent of it and can be dragged outside it.

You cannot drag an object from one page to another, even if it is not nested in the original page's ptf. To move an object from one page to another, you must use the clipboard to cut it from its original page and paste it on the destination page.

Interaction between objects

As we have seen, you may create one frame inside another. And one frame may overlap another. So what happens to the contents of frames when they are laid one on top of another?

Adding new frames is rather like pasting scraps into a scrapbook, one on top of another. The frames you have added in later overlie those you introduced earlier and therefore usually hide them. But the following exceptions apply.

You can rearrange the order of the objects if you wish. The Send Behind option on the Object menu sends the currently active object behind the other objects you have added so it is concealed by them. The Bring Forward option brings the active object to the to the front so it overlies all other objects. But the ptf cannot be brought forwards; it is always at the back of the page; all other objects are in front of it.

This is some text which is here to demonstrate the way in which frames repel text beneath them.

If a text or picture frame overlies a text frame, the text in that frame is repelled, that is to say, it is reformatted so that it flows around the newly introduced frame and none of it is hidden. If there is space on either side of the newly introduced frame, the text will be laid on one side of it only, the side that offers the greater width.

This is some text which is here to demonstrate the way in which frames repel text beneath them.

However, if the newly introduced frame has been made transparent, the text beneath will not be repelled,

An illustration of text repulsion

and because the overlying frame is transparent, you should be able to see the text (or some of it) underneath. This allows you to create special effects in which an image is superimposed over text. If you want a graphic superimposed on text, you will certainly get better results if the text is placed in a transparent frame overlying the graphics.

> This text has been deliberately placed in a transparent text frame so that the graphic beneath it is plainly visible. If the graphic frame had been made transparent and laid over the text, the text beneath the solid part of the graphic would have been concealed.

Text in a transparent frame is still legible when superimposed over graphics

Lines behave like transparent frames - they do not repel text beneath them and can even be laid straight over text.

Borders

Text and picture frames can be given decorative borders. You make the frame active and select Frame Border from the object menu. A scrolling selector offers a number of border styles ranging from a plain solid line to some highly ornate types; not all may be available on your system; since border definitions use precious memory space, on smaller computer systems there

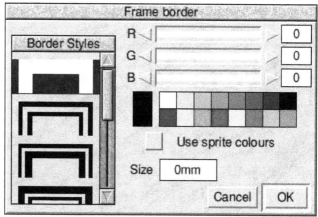

The Frame Border dialogue box

may be only a limited selection. The currently selected style is shown in inverse video. The dialogue box offers a writable choice of border width in the currently selected units besides the usual selection of border colours.

The width of the border is added to the outside of the frame to which it is being applied. If there is insufficient room for the specified border (because it would project outside a parent frame) an error message will be given. Of course, this error will occur with any border width (apart from 0) if the frame is hard against the edge of a parent frame. To remove a border from a frame, simply set its size to 0.

You can design your own border styles and add them to the selection available. See the Ovation User Manual for further information on this.

Hints and Tips

If you need to create a large number of frames or lines, click Adjust on the appropriate Ovation tool. This will keep the tool active after the creation of each new frame or line. If you click with Select, after the creation of each new object the text entry tool is automatically reselected.

When you are scaling sprites in picture frames, you must be careful about the scaling factor you choose. If the document is to be printed on a 300 or 600 dots-per-inch printer, you are recommended to use a factor which is a multiple of 90 per cent, such as 30, 45, 90 or 180%. If you are using a 360 dots-per-inch printer, you are recommended to use a factor which is a multiple of 100 per cent such as 25, 50, 100 or 200%. If you use other factors, you may find that unsightly fringes and chequerboard patterns appear in the printout.

Avoid positioning two frames beside side each other inside a text frame in which contains text beneath the frames. You may find that, even though the bottom edges of the two frames appear to be level, there is a discrepancy between them which interferes with the position of the text beneath causing it to begin or end in the middle of the page. Instead, create an additional text or picture frame and nest both frames within it.

3 Planning your document

So far we have looked at the typing of text and the use of the text frames, picture frames and lines which make up an Ovation document. If you have been experimenting with Ovation as you read, probably you have already created a collection of experimental documents which make use of the wide range of effects that Ovation offers.

If you intend to use Ovation for a serious task such as the production of a brochure or magazine for your school, club, church or business, you will need to exercise some restraint in your page layouts. While there should still be ample room for creativity and variety, any multi-page document needs consistency to lend it a distinctive 'character' of its own. One way to ensure this consistency is to use the same page layout (for example, the same number, width and height of columns) and the same body typeface (that is the typeface used for printing ordinary text) and subheading typefaces throughout the document. To add variety, however, main headings may be allowed to use different fonts and styles to suit the situation.

If each page used a different layout and different body text styles, the finished publication would be - frankly - a mess. It would look like like a motley collection of pages drawn from different sources and readers would gain the impression that its Editor was an unruly character. Ovation contains many powerful tools that not only keep your document orderly and consistent, but also save you much tedious work.

Just as a builder beginning work on a house has a set of plans which show him how the various structural members fit together, so a publisher considers the contents and style of a proposed new publication long before initiating production proper. In the same way some initial planning of any Ovation document will pay huge dividends in time and convenience during production itself.

You need to consider, for instance, who are the intended readers and, if the document is to be reproduced in quantity, who will print it and by what process. For example, if it is a club or church magazine on a tight budget, and if it is reproduced by photocopying on a machine that takes A4 paper only, then your page size is limited to A5 (since A4 folds to A5). If the document uses A4 pages and contains long articles, you should use a two- or three-column layout, since wide columns of small print are difficult to read. If you are using A4 pages and have many short items such as news snippets or small ads, then a three- or even a four-column layout is desirable.

These multi-column layouts could be set up by dragging out a separate text frame for each column, carefully manipulating them to the same height, width and separation and then linking them as necessary. But that is both tedious and unnecessary since Ovation will do it all for you instantly by means of its master pages. Any alteration of the master pages, however, should ideally be made at the start of production; changes at later stages, especially if the document includes many frames and lines, are very tedious.

Using the master pages

When you create a new document by clicking Select on the Ovation icon, by default your document is A4 size with a single column ptf. You may resize the ptf by dragging its handles, but if your document runs on to a second page, you will find that on the new page the ptf has reverted to the original size. That is because new pages in Ovation take their layout not from the previous page, but from a page layout stored in memory. That page layout is called the master page and you can see it and edit it by selecting the Show Master Pages option from the Page menu (via the main menu). Although you may resize the ptf on any page, this does not affect the master page and so all new pages will follow the pattern of the master page.

If the default page layout is not suitable for your document, instead of clicking Select on the Ovation icon, click Menu on it, and then choose the New Document option (or with an existing document open press Ctrl-N).

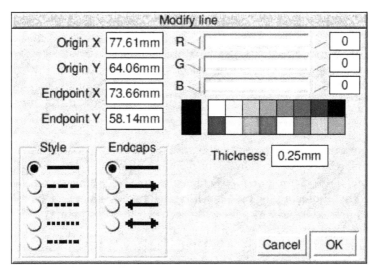

The Modify Line Dialogue Box

This dialogue box allows you to design a new page layout to your own precise specification. First you choose your page size. Ovation offers a choice of six popular page sizes including A4 and A5. You click on the 'radio button' for your preferred size. If you are uncertain of the measurements of any of the standard sizes offered, click on it and the measurements appear in the panes at the foot of the column. If you wish to use a non-standard size, click on the Other button and enter your choice of width and height.

You are also offered a choice of Orientation: portrait or landscape. Portrait means that the longer axis is vertical, as in most portrait paintings. Most magazines and books have portrait orientation. In landscape orientation the longer axis is horizontal as in most landscape paintings. Some brochures use landscape orientation. When you change the orientation, you see the width and height figures change places.

The Margins pane is concerned with the area of the page that is actually used for printing. Top and Bottom control the areas that are left empty at the top and bottom of the page. Similarly Left and Right control the empty space along the left and right edges of the page. If you click on the Double Sided button, however, Ovation will work with double-page spreads which include separate left and right master pages. Left and Right change to Outer and Inner controlling the outermost margins and the innermost margins respectively. It is common practice to make the inner margins wider than the outer to allow for the binding.

If you make the margins so small that nearly all the page area is used, you should check that your printer will be able to handle all the printed area. Before undertaking any serious production work, load your printer driver, select Show Print Margin from the View menu and check that the ptf does not stray into the printer margin (shown in pale grey). If it does, but only along one or two edges, you may be able to correct this by adjusting the printer X and Y offsets on the Print Setup option from the File menu. If your printed area is just too big for the printer, you can use the print scale option option also on Print Setup to print at a reduced size. But this will affect the printed size of both text and graphics. And if you have used sprite graphics, you may find that these require careful rescaling to avoid unsightly fringing.

The Header and Footer are reserved areas within the ptf. The header is an area set aside at the top of the ptf and the footer an area at the foot. By default these are set to 0 mm and so effectively do not exist. But if you are creating a magazine or a booklet, you will probably want to use either or both. In a book (in this one for instance) the book's title often appears in the left-hand header and the chapter title in the right-hand header. In a magazine you may prefer to place the magazine title in the left-hand footer and the issue number and cover date in the right-hand footer. Page numbers are usually placed in headers or footers. So, if

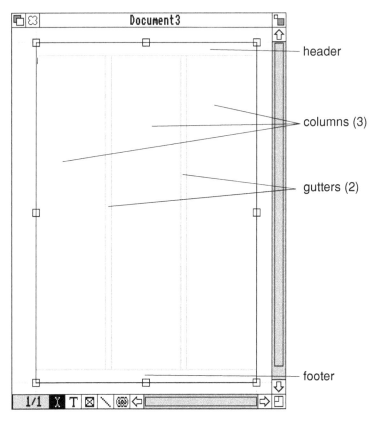

A three-column layout with a header and a footer.

your document needs to use headers or footers, you should work out how much space you will need at this stage.

The Guidelines pane is concerned with columns. By default the ptf is set up with one column which is the full width of the ptf. But you may specify as many columns as you wish. You may also specify the gutter width, that is, the space that is left between adjacent columns; by default this is 5mm. Ovation does not allow you to specify the column width directly; it divides the remaining space between the columns after allowing for the margins and gutters.

Although all measurements in the New Document dialogue box are shown initially in mm, you may enter measurements in inches or points if you prefer. Simply delete the 'mm' and enter 'in' or 'pt' after the figure.

When you have entered the vital data for your new document, click on OK or press Return. A window will be opened showing the first page of your new document.

The multi-column layout works in the same way as the single-column text frames with which we are familiar. Pressing the Enter key takes the caret to the top of the next column, whether that is on the same page or the next one.

You will find that you cannot take the caret into the header or footer. To place text in the header or footer you must access the master pages themselves via the Page menu. This will call up a page display exactly like the document window itself except that the word Master precedes the document title in the title bar. If you selected Double sided in the New Document dialogue box, you will find that there are two master pages suffixed L and R for left and right.

In the master page window, you will find that the conditions in the document window are reversed: you cannot type in the normal ptf, but you can type in the header and footer. Indeed, the header and the footer behave rather like normal unlinked text frames. The full range of fonts, styles and formats is available to you.

Wherever you want the current page number to appear in documents, place the caret and press Insert. On the master pages the page number is shown as a hash sign (#); it can be marked and treated in every respect like normal text. In the document window this will be replaced by the current page number. Remember that if you want the page number in a left corner on left pages and a right corner in right pages, you must format the page number so it is ranged right on the right-hand pages. Anything that you type in the header or footer of a master page will be reproduced on all pages based on that master page, including pages that already exist.

There are other changes that you can make to master pages. You can introduce text frames, picture frames or lines anywhere on the master pages. This is useful if you wish to include, say, a motif in each header. Objects that appear on pages because they were included in the master pages are normal in every respect; they may be moved, edited or deleted in the normal way. You can also change the size of the ptf by dragging its handles just as you can in the document window. But these changes only take effect on new pages that are created subsequently. They are not applied to pages that already exist.

You may also introduce guidelines in your master pages (or in the document window itself). These are dotted lines across or down the page which appear on the screen, but not in printouts. They help you to lay out the page. Frames or lines will snap on to a guideline and this helps you to ensure that items are aligned neatly. To introduce a guideline you must have the rulers visible. Take the pointer into a ruler, move it to the position where you want the guideline and press Select. You can subsequently drag the guideline with Adjust. To remove a guideline, simply drag it over the edge of the page. Guidelines created on the master pages, like frames or lines, appear only on subsequently created pages.

You can force changes of the master pages on to existing pages, but the operation is a drastic one. If, say, you have already created pages 1 to 4 when you decide to redesign the master pages, you may choose to delete pages 1 to 4 (from the Page menu). Everything that was on pages 1 to 4 will be lost except for the text in the ptf; this alone will remain in memory and, after the deletion, new pages will be created and the text will be introduced into the ptfs. Of course, these new pages will take their layout from your redesigned master pages. But any other objects that were on your original pages 1 to 4 will be lost.

When this kind of drastic action is necessary, it is useful first to save the original document and then reload it leaving the original window open, so you now have windows open on to two identical but independent documents. Do your redesign and page deletion in one window and then transfer all the lost frames and lines from the other using the clipboard. When you are sure that you have transferred everything, delete the original window.

Chapters

Ovation allows you to divide your document into what it calls chapters. The number of the current chapter is shown in the bottom left-hand corner of the document (or master page) window, before the page number and separated from it by an oblique (/). If your document is not divided into chapters, Ovation regards it as all one chapter, numbered 1.

Unlike the chapters in a book which are generally uniform in style and layout, the chapters in an Ovation document may each have a different style and layout, because each chapter has its own separate master page (or pair of master pages if double-sided). This facility is especially useful if you are creating a document which has several distinct sections. It may, for example, be a magazine which has a news section with a three-column layout, followed by a feature article section having a two-column layout, followed by a small-ads section having a four-column layout. Clearly each section will need its own separate pair of master pages. Of course, you could create the magazine as three separate files, each havings its own pair of master pages, but then if you inserted a pair of extra pages in the first section, you would have to remember to renumber the pages in the other two sections; if you use one document divided into chapters, the page numbering will look after itself.

To create a new chapter select the New Chapter option from the Page menu. Moving right on this option offers a choice of position before or after the current chapter. If you simply click Select on the New Chapter option itself, the new chapter will be added after the current chapter. On the screen a black bar between pages indicates a division between chapters.

A blank first page will be created in your new chapter. Its layout will initially follow that of the earlier chapter, but you can redesign it as you wish. Click select on that first page to place the caret in it. From the page menu select Show Master Pages. There will now be a set of master pages for each chapter, the chapters being separated by a black bar as in the document window. You can modify the master pages as you please except that you cannot change the page size; that was fixed when you first created the document. If you wish to change the margins or the number of columns in the master page layout, from the Page menu select the Page Guidelines option. This produces a dialogue box consisting of the Margins and Guidelines panes of the New Document dialogue box which we met earlier. Changes made will apply to the selected master page only and therefore only to the chapter to which it relates, that is the chapter indicated in the bottom left-hand corner of the window.

When your document contains more than one chapter, Ctrl-up (or Home) and Ctrl-down move the caret to the start and finish of the current chapter only; they will not take the caret past a chapter division. To move the caret into another chapter, change the view using the sliders or the Page Up or Page Down keys, move the pointer into the new chapter and click Select to place the caret there.

The text in different chapters constitutes separate stories. Select All applied in one chapter does not select text in other chapters. A search in one chapter will not find the sequence sought in another chapter.

On the Page menu there is an option named Modify Chapter which is useful even if your document is not divided into chapters. It it is concerned with page numbering. It allows you to change the number of the first page of the chapter (and of course subsequent pages are renumbered to maintain the sequence) and the format of the page numbers. This is valuable if you use Ovation to write a book in which the chapters are stored as separate documents (perhaps because the whole book would be too big a document to load into your computer). You can ensure that each separate chapter begins with the page number that follows the last page of the previous chapter.

There is also a Delete Chapter option. This drastic operation is only available if your document contains more than one chapter. It deletes the chapter in which the caret is placed. All text and graphics in the pages contained in the current chapter are lost, so use this facility with care.

Paragraph styles

Another facility which helps to give your document consistency and saves much time and effort is Ovation's comprehensive paragraph style handling.

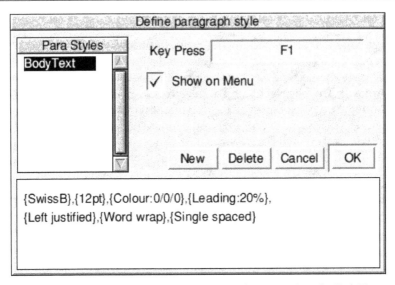

The paragraph style specification for the default paragraph style, BodyText

Remember that in Ovation a paragraph is any sequence of text delimited by Return characters (or by the start or end of the story). So a chapter heading, a figure caption or a subheading like the one preceding this paragraph counts as a paragraph.

Each paragraph has a style and each style has a name. The default style is called 'BodyText' and every Ovation document includes a style by that name. BodyText is the style that is in force if you click Select on the Ovation icon to open a new document window and start typing text in it immediately. It will be the only style available (since you have not added any others) and you can read its specification by choosing the Para. Style option from the main menu and selecting the first item, Edit Style. The pane at the bottom of the box shows that the default BodyText style uses the font family Homerton (this may vary depending on the selection of fonts available) and since neither Bold nor Italic is included in the definition, the Medium variety will be used. The type size is 12pt, the colour is black (0/0/0 means no red, no green and no blue), the leading is 20%, the text is justified to left margin only, word wrap is turned on and single spacing is selected.

The Paragraph Styles menu before a lot has been added. The style featured, BodyText, is as defined in the screenshot on the previous page.

Any or all of these choices may be edited to suit your requirements. Moreover, you may define up to 31 more paragraph styles. For example, when this booklet was prepared using Ovation, BodyText was edited changing the font to Paladin, the type size to 14 pt, the leading to 18% and the format to justified (both margins). And five more paragraph styles were defined and given meaningful names. A tick appears against the style currently in force, that is, at the caret.

The value of paragraph styles is that they allow you to change font, type size, any style aspects and any format aspects in one operation, maybe even with a single keypress. For example, in this booklet subheadings such as the one on the previous page differ from BodyText in five respects: the font is Paladin Bold, the size is 18pt but with Horizontal Scale set to 90%, the leading is 20% and the justification is left margin only. Without definable paragraph styles, the subheadings would be typed in standard BodyText style. Each subheading would then need to be marked and those five changes selected individually, a tedious job. But Ovation's paragraph style system allows you either to select a style from the menu while typing or to change the style of a finished paragraph by placing the caret in it (or by including it in a marked spread of several paragraphs) and then selecting the required style from the menu. If the required style has a function key assigned to it, a press on that key will have the same effect as clicking on the menu option.

To define a new paragraph style click on Para. Style and then on Edit Style. The dialogue box shown in Figure 3.3 will appear and will contain the definition of whichever style is currently selected. Click on New at the the top of the box. A small dialogue box will appear in which you enter the name you wish to give your new style; it is sensible to give it a name which reflects its use. It also includes a pane labelled Based On followed by the name of the currently selected style. You may delete this and insert the name of any other style provided of course that it exists; choose the one that is most similar to the style you wish to create. Obviously, if your document only has BodyText, you must base your new style on that. Next you may assign a function key to your new style if you wish. You cannot use F1 (which is BodyText) nor F3 to F5 nor F12 since RISC OS assigns special functions to these, but F2 and F6 to F11 may be allocated to paragraph styles. The paragraph style definition at the foot of the box will now contain the definition of the 'based on' style. You modify it by clicking Menu with the pointer in the dialogue box. This leads to a short menu of four items: Font, Size, Style and Format. Each of these leads to the menu of the same name; we met them all in Chapter 1. Choosing items from these four menus you assign your choice of font, type size, style and format to your new paragraph style. When all is correct, click on OK. The dialogue box will disappear and your new style will be added to the list of paragraph styles for your document.

If you are dissatisfied with a paragraph style definition, you may edit it at any time. The procedure is the same as creating a new one, but select the style you wish to edit first and don't click on New. When you finally click on OK, Ovation will work its way through the entire document applying your changes to all text in that paragraph style. This may make a considerable difference to the length of the document, especially if a font or type size has been changed. For example, illustrations may no longer be near the text to which they relate.

The Reset option on the Para. Style menu removes local styles from text. For example, in the paragraph above this one, there is a solitary example of a local style~the word Ovation in the fourth line is in italics. Italics are not a part of the normal definition of BodyText; this style was applied individually to that word making it a local style. If the caret were placed in that paragraph and the Reset option applied, BodyText would be applied again to the paragraph, but local styles would be removed, so that word would revert to the default Paladin Roman.

Stylesheets

You may wish to use the same master pages and paragraph styles for more than one document. For example, if you have created the first issue of a magazine, you probably expect many more issues to follow; these will use the same layout and paragraph styles. Of course, you could create the second issue by loading the first and then deleting all the text and graphics from it, but that would be tedious. Ovation will do that for you in the form of a stylesheet. Load the document whose style you wish to follow and from the File menu choose the sixth item, Save Stylesheet. Save the file to disc in the normal way. You use the stylesheet by dragging it on to the Ovation icon or double clicking on it, provided the computer knows where to find Ovation. This will open a new document window having the same master pages and paragraph styles as the original document, but otherwise empty, ready for you to insert new text and graphics.

Incidentally, you can transfer all the paragraph style definitions from one document to another as follows. Save a stylesheet from the source document to disc. Open the Edit Paragraph Styles window in the destination document. Drag the saved stylesheet from the directory display into the list of styles. Ovation will ask if you wish to overwrite styles and you must click on Discard or the operation will be abandoned. Then click on OK in the Edit Paragraph Styles window. The styles from the source document will be merged with those from the destination document. If any styles have the same name (and inevitably there will be two BodyTexts) the one from the source document will overwrite that from the destination document. This operation does not affect master page layouts.

4 Other Facilities

This final chapter describes some of Ovation's facilities that have not been covered in earlier chapters. It also tells you about printing your document.

Checking your spelling

Spelling mistakes and typing errors create a poor impression on any reader and they seem all the more out of place when they occur in a document that has been carefully laid out. Ovation's spelling checker helps you to eliminate this kind of fault.

An integral part of Ovation, the spelling checker is loaded automatically if your computer has 2 Mbs or more of RAM. You cannot use this feature on a 1 Mb machine.

It works by looking up each word you have typed in one or more lists called dictionaries. If the word occurs in a dictionary, it is regarded as correct, otherwise it is suspect. The dictionaries are kept in a directory called Dictionary in the !Ovation application. Two dictionaries are supplied with Ovation, but only one, called !MainDict is concerned with the spelling (the other one, !HyphDict, is concerned with hyphenation).

To use the spelling checker select the final option on the main menu, Spell. This leads to a submenu of four options, three of which are spelling check routines and the fourth is concerned with maintenance of the dictionaries. Check Story causes Ovation to work through the current story (that is, the one containing the caret or marked text) checking each word. Check Word checks only the word containing the caret (or the first word in a marked area). Continuous Check checks each word you type; Ovation waits until you finish a word with a space or

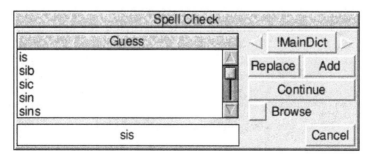

The spell check dialogue box.

a punctuation mark, otherwise unfinished words would be repeatedly signalled as suspect.

All three routines operate on the 'no news is good news' principle. That is to say, when the word being checked is found in a dictionary no action is taken. The panel in the bottom left-hand corner contains the suspect word as it appears in the Ovation document; also, in the document window the suspect word is highlighted. In the large Guess panel the spelling checker displays a selection of words from the dictionary which closely resemble the suspect word. If one of these is the word you intended to use, double-click Select on it to replace the misspelt word. Single-clicking Select places the selection in the lower panel, where it can be edited before clicking on Replace to replace the misspelt word. This is useful if you agree that the suspect word is incorrect, but the correct word does not appear in the Guess panel.

Inevitably, sometimes the spelling checker will query a word that is correctly spelt but which is not in any dictionary, especially if it is a technical term, a foreign word or the name of a person, place or product. When this happens, click on Continue to resume work without taking any further action. Actually, Ovation does take some action: it adds the queried word to a temporary dictionary so that further occurrences of it in the same story will not be signalled as suspect. Alternatively, you may add the word to !MainDict or to a dictionary of your own making. To add the word to !MainDict click on Add. At the end of the spellcheck session you will be asked to confirm that you wish this and any other new words to be added to the dictionary.

If you choose the Continuous Check facility, the dialogue box is not used. The computer simply beeps whenever you type a word that is suspect.

The fourth item in the Spell menu, Dictionary, allows you to load, edit, save and delete dictionaries. You could create a specialist dictionary of, say, technical terms or the names of people with whom you have frequent dealings. If you load this, it will be searched for any suspect words not in !MainDict; this prevents the spelling checker from flagging these words each time it finds them in a document. For further information on this see the Ovation User Manual.

One word of warning. The spelling checker will only find a spelling or typing error if it forms a word that is not in any dictionary. Some errors result in words that exist although wrong in their present context. So, if you intended to type 'beam' but actually typed 'bean', the error would not be found because 'bean' is a legitimate word. Ultimately there is no alternative to scrupulous manual checking of documents.

You will ultimately need some form of thesaurus: Word Hound, by Ian Palmer, would seem to do the trick.

Special text effects

You may wonder how to create some of the special text effects you have seen in magazines and newspapers. These include text at an angle including 90 degrees, text with different outline and fill colours, text that is upside down or mirror imaged or in a circle and text with a shadow. You cannot apply any of these effects to text in Ovation's text frames, but you can create these effects in picture frames.

There are two ways in which you can apply an angle to a line of text. The simplest is to use Draw to create the text as a text object, then select the text object and rotate it to the required angle. Finally, save the Draw file into an Ovation picture frame.

Some of the manipulations of text converted to graphics in Draw.

An alternate method is to convert your text to graphics. The conversion itself does not change the outward appearance of the text, but when it has been converted it can be subjected to the same manipulations and transformations as any other 'path objects'. These include rotation, inversion, mirror imaging and changes of outline and fill colours.

Font manipulation packages such as Typestudio offer an even wider range of exciting effects such as block shadows, graded shadows and text that follows the course of a line which may be curved or even a circle. The line itself can be made invisible. Typestudio also offers 'moulds', which constrain converted text (or other path objects, for that matter) to fit between a pair of lines.

Some of the text effects possible using TypeStudio

The Print dialogue box.

Printing your work

Before you can print your work you must load the printer driver for your printer and ensure that the printer is ready. Then press the Print key.

The Print dialogue box is concerned with what is printed and how much of it. The first option, Copies, determines the number of copies printed, which may be up to 9999. Beware! Printing is a slow process and printing multiple copies may tie up your computer and printer for hours. If you need many copies of a document, print out just one and photocopy it.

You may print the whole document or any spread of pages. By default All is selected; this prints the whole document. To print just part click on the From:/To: buttons and enter the start and finish chapter/page numbers. To print a single page from a multi-page document enter that page's number in both From: and To: panels. Whether you are printing the whole document or part of it, you have the further option of printing just the odd or the even pages, which is useful when you are printing on both sides of the paper.

Towards the bottom of the dialogue box are several further options. Reverse Print prints the pages in reverse order, that is, from the highest page number down to the lowest. This may be useful when you are printing on both sides of the paper or using printers which deposit printed pages face upwards.

Collate controls the print sequence when printing multiple copies of a multi-page document. When selected, it cycles through the whole document once for each copy required, printing single pages, so that pages are printed in the correct sequence 1, 2, 3... 1, 2, 3... etc. On some printers, especially laser printers, however, this will greatly increase the printing time. If not selected, the whole document is cycled once, with multiple copies of each page being printed together, thus: 1, 1, 1... 2, 2, 2... 3, 3, 3...

Pause Between Pages forces the computer to wait at the end of each page. This is for use with printers which require each sheet to be fed in manually.

Print Pictures is normally selected. If you disable it, the contents of picture frames are not printed which speeds up printing and saves ink. This is useful if you require a proof copy of a document so that the text can be checked before undertaking the final 'proper' printout.

Draft Print produces a very rapid printout using the printer's built-in typefaces rather than outline fonts. Effects such as bold and italics are reproduced, but otherwise the printout does not reflect the page layout. It is useful for checking that the text is correct.

Merge is used in mail merge and will be considered later.

When you have selected the required options click on OK or press Return to start printing.

The time taken to print the document depends on the complexity of the document, the type of printer, the graphics resolution set on the printer and, above all, the memory available in the computer. The more memory the faster the printing. If you are using a 1Mb and a RISC OS 2 printer driver machine, you may even get a message stating that there is insufficient memory available to print the document. This is because the document is printed as graphics and memory is needed in the computer to build up an image of the document at the printer's graphics resolution.

If this happens, don't despair. You can release memory for the printer driver in the following ways: (1) quit any unwanted applications or any unwanted Ovation documents; (2) change the screen mode to mode 0 (click menu on the palette icon and enter 0 for mode; don't be deterred by the appearance of the screen, the printout is unaffected); (3) having ensured that the printer driver is correctly set up, quit it. This may sound counter-productive, but the front end that appears on the icon bar takes 64 Kb. Quitting it releases that space while still leaving the module in memory that is actually needed for printing.

Reproducing your work

If you want to distribute your document to a wide readership, this will affect some decisions you make concerning the printout. Much will depend on the type of printer you have and the method used to reproduce the document. If you have a laser printer, this may well give acceptable quality for reproduction by photocopying or litho printing. But if you use graphics or coloured text, you must carefully consider the printer's resolution. Most laser printers offer a true resolution of 300 dpi (dots per inch); some also offer a quasi-high resolution of 600 dpi. This genuinely prints 600 dots per inch, but the dots are the same size as those used at 300 dpi. Consequently tints, that is the rendering of areas of grey or colour, will appear too dark and are prone to unsightly streaking as adjacent dots merge into each other. Moreover, many photocopiers and litho platemakers cannot satisfactorily reproduce tints at 600 dpi, but most can reproduce them at 300 dpi. Do experiment to see what the equipment available to you can do, but be prepared to find that the reproduced document looks best when the original printout was at 300 dpi.

If you have only a dot-matrix printer, you may consider that its quality is not adequate for reproduction, since all reproduction processes tend to make shortcomings in the original document all the more obvious. Don't worry, all is not lost. If you know someone who has a laser printer, he may be able to do a printout on his machine for you, even if he does not have an Acorn computer. The easiest means is to set up for yourself (within !Printers) a Postscript printer driver, and set that to print to file. If your friend does not have a postscript printer, consider the purchase of a PDF creator (either on their computer or your own) which will provide document portability.

From the MS DOS prompt they can be printed by issuing a command such as PRINT A:page1 when page1 is the name of the file on floppy drive A. The printing process is a 'background task' so the PC can be used for other purposes at the same time. This still applies to current versions of Windows: they may need to specify the path of the printer.

If you want truly professional quality a typesetting company such as Micro Laser Designs - at www.mld.co.uk - will be able to help.

Mail merge

Mail merge allows you to print multiple copies of a document in which the details vary from copy to copy. It is used by businesses, schools and clubs to send personalised letters to customers, pupils' parents or guardians and members.

To do a mail merge first prepare a file containing the individual data with which you wish to personalise your letter. The file should be a standard RISC OS text file created using Edit or another text editor or created in Ovation and saved using the Save as Text option. It should contain a number of entries, one for each letter you wish to send, separated by Return characters. That is, each entry is a line or paragraph. Each entry is divided into fields, separated by commas. If you need to include a comma as part of the data in a field, enclose the entire field in quotation marks. A file written by a teacher regarding some of his pupils might be as follows:

```
Brown, Brian, 14 High Street, Longtown, Oldshire OLD 9XX
Jones, John, 36 The Avenue, Longtown, Oldshire OLD 9YZ
Smith, Susan, 5 Acacia Grove, Longtown, Oldshire OLD 9TU
```

When you compose the letter in Ovation, at each point where you need to merge data press Ctrl-I. A Merge dialogue box will appear in which you enter the number of the field to be merged at that point. This appears in the Ovation document as normal text enclosed in square brackets taking the form [Merge x] where x is the number of the field you requested. You can delete this instruction with a single press of the Delete key if you wish.

When you print your document, click on the Merge button in the Print dialogue box and enter the file name containing the data to be merged. Ovation will now print as many copies of the document as there are entries in the file and will substitute each Merge x instruction with the data in the field identified from the current entry. Of course, your document may use each field as many times as you wish and in any order you wish.

The teacher who composed the data file shown above might compose a letter which begins as follows:

```
The parents or guardians of [Merge 2] [Merge 1],
[Merge 3],
[Merge 4],
[Merge 5]

4th May 1993

Dear friends,

[Merge 2] will begin studying for the GCSE examinations
in September. Our school offers a wide choice of subjects.
In order to help you and [Merge 2] to make the most
suitable choice a meeting has been arranged in the School
Hall at 7.30pm on 18th May at which the Headmaster and a
Careers Adviser from Longshire Education Committee will be
present...
```

The first time this document is printed the Merge instructions will be substituted by the appropriate fields from the first entry in the data file. The letter will therefore be printed as follows:

```
The parents or guardians of Brian Brown,
14 High Street,
Longtown,
Oldshire OLD9XX

4th May 1993

Dear friends,

Brian will begin studying GCSE subjects in September. Our
school offers a wide choice of subjects. In order to help you
and Brian to make the most suitable choice a meeting has
been arranged in the School Hall at 7.30pm on 18th May at
which the Headmaster and a Careers Adviser from Longshire
Education Committee will be present...
```

You will see that Ovation has automatically reformatted the text where necessary. Where the data in fields is appreciably longer than the Merge instructions, you may need to ensure that there is sufficient free space at the end of the page, or your letters may need more pages than you allowed for.

Incidentally, when writing letters and memos you can use Ctrl-Insert to type today's date automatically at the caret position. Shift-Insert types the current time and Shift-Ctrl-Insert types the date followed by the time. See the User Manual for ways in which you can edit the format in which these appear.